The Song

of a

Soul

By

Alban M. Emley

SCIENCE OF MIND PUBLICATIONS
Los Angeles, California

SCIENCE OF MIND PUBLICATIONS EDITION
January 1973

Printed by arrangement with
Mrs. Edith T. Emley

Published by SCIENCE OF MIND PUBLICATIONS
3251 West Sixth Street, Los Angeles, California 90020
ISBN 0-911336-45-1

Preface

The Song of a Soul! A wonderful thought, because it is the song that every human being must sing upon the wheel of life.

As the inspiring words of Alban Emley are read, one senses that the wheel has spun many times for Mr. Emley. In its spinning he has reached the light of Cosmic Consciousness.

As an Adept gives of his wisdom to the pupil at his feet, the simple and beautiful lines of the book guide the inquiring mind into avenues of higher realization.

Whoever is so fortunate as to hear the overtones of the Cosmos in the whisper of leaves, and the Chorus of the Stars in the warble of a bird, will recognize the Divine Melody as his own Great Song.

In this book you will find a beacon that will inspire you into bringing to mankind the beautiful song that is within your own soul.

— FRANCES K. CHAMBERLAIN

The Song of a Soul

I

Voice From The Silence

To know the joy and serenity of Infinite Peace, go into the secret places of the heart and close the door.

Still the mind.

Let it sleep.

Sink deep into unfathomed seas of space and time.

Lose the consciousness of Self and its multitude of woes.

Hear the Voice where there is no voice.

Listen to Words where there is no speech.

Probe the inner depths where thought ceases and apprehension begins.

Find the realm where the deep stillness rests within a serene and Infinite Peace that surpasses human understanding.

Sink into the soft darkness where there is no awareness of body or mind or thought.

You will hear the Voice that whispers in the silent realm of your innermost Being.

Listen and be at peace!

Let Stillness enfold you within its velvet depth.

Power will be with you, and wisdom and joy.

You hear the murmur of Ages that contains every movement and all knowledge.

You remain in the blissful Silence undisturbed and untouched by the clamor of Men.

Your inner, higher consciousness becomes attuned to the rushing, resounding song of Creation, the song of all eternity, the song the stars sang together in the gray dawn of Cosmic Day, the song of a Soul.

To enter the Silence, turn inward, then look upward and outward.

Approach the mystic veil that lies beyond your thought and afar above the turmoil of earthly things.

The inner meaning of Life unfolds by slow degrees, like the rays of a lingering dawn.

You see only the first refractions from the Light that appears with Cosmic Day.

Peering upward from the soil wherein your roots are fixed, you behold the gray of early morn.

Beyond is the pure, white, raying, flashing, pulsating Light of Creation, where all is motion, energy, harmony, peace and joy.

The Plan of God unfolds in measured tread.

Its movement is slow.

It pauses as though in contemplation, then surges onward again, and the world is torn in the travail of birth anew.

An Age begins, and chaos reigns before the new is established.

Every movement is fixed and certain.

It was determined in the Infinite Plan.

Yet, in peaceful, ordered motion, Men find turmoil and despair, for they are as Beings underneath the surface of the sea.

They feel the lashing of the waves, but neither see nor comprehend the Breath that moves them, nor the Light beyond.

In the birth of new things confusion and turmoil comes to Mankind, but not to God who ordained all.

The loves and hatreds and fears and struggles of men are but fleeting, ephemeral whirlings within the stream of Life that moves and changes and endures throughout eternity.

They are here today.

Tomorrow they will be forgotten as they are absorbed and smoothed within the current of the mighty stream that flows forever into the Unknown.

The language of Men is confined to the sphere of written word and vocal sound.

It fails when you reach into the depths of the Stillness.

There you do not think.

You apprehend.

You do not reason.

You know!

You are in a realm where there is neither mental effort nor emotional response.

You touch the etheric plane of Boundless Light.

Look up.

See beyond!

Understanding comes not from gazing into the turmoil of earth.

It is found within the whisper that echoes deep into the silent chambers of the Unknown.

Seek not to solve the mystery of the Unmanifest, for it lies infinitely beyond the realm of finite mind.

You cannot grasp it.

You can do no more than brush the hem of its garment.

Yet you may catch faint glimmerings of Cosmic Truth, and know that joy and pain and laughter and tears are but passing phases of a mighty Force that works in peace and harmony.

Knowing this, you stand firmly on the path of Conscious Being, the mighty arc of evolution.

Creation is like the shining of a Sun beyond the sun.

It pierces through the living blackness and loses itself in the vastness of eternal and never-ending space.

Human response to Cosmic impulse comes slowly, as a gift that is grudgingly bestowed.

The suffering of the world would turn to gladness if Men could raise their eyes to the Light and understand.

There is choice for them; choice, not only of path, but also of direction.

The Cosmic Tides move steadily into the Unknown, and the pace and measure and purpose and destination are decreed by One who fashions all things by Infinite Will.

The Plan of God, in its infinite perfection, is hidden from Men by the smoke of the wildly burning fires they kindle. Yet Men are engaged in performing their part of the Scheme of Things in accordance with Divine Law. Few indeed are slothful and unwilling servants.

For a little while, they must struggle and weep in the blinding process of Becoming, as they go dashing thither and yon without conscience and without aim.

Even so, they are firmly established in the Stream of Life that moves toward one objective, and one only: Consummation.

The seething, surging movements of Cosmic Creation are all about you.

Feel them.

Heed them.

Go with them into the peaceful current that leads to the Light.

The earth is but a cosmic atom whirling among a grand array of worlds and stars.

The hopes and joys and sorrows and pain of Men are but momentary, emotional surgings that move onward and leave no trace within the Cosmic Tides.

They seem important today.

Tomorrow they will be absorbed into the realm of the infinitely small, like a measure of salt dissolved in the waters of a mighty sea.

Yet it is through them that Mankind unfolds into a higher state of conscious Being.

Look beyond, not at them, if you would draw nearer to the consciousness of Him that sent the Life Wave upward and outward in the spinning and weaving of atoms and worlds and stars and human souls.

The Way that has no turning and no ending lies at your feet.

It branches into many paths, and each of them leads to God who fashioned all.

The one you choose is of no importance.

Your only concern is the Great Objective. Every path ends in One as you reach the Light.

Take courage and go forward into the New, which to you must ever be the uncertain and the unknown.

Cast aside the chains that hold you to the past, and speed consciousness toward the glory of the day that is to be.

Never can you know the Plan of God, nor can you see the wonders of the path that lies before you.

It reaches far beyond the veil that hangs as a cloud before human vision.

It is like a moving mist that cannot be pierced or transcended, for it travels with you.

Trust God, and see the fullness of Life unfolding before you as the veil recedes.

Listen and look.

Watch and pray.

The mighty movements of the Cosmos are beyond the awareness of the finite mind. From fragments and reflections you gain understanding.

The joys and tears and coilings and turnings of Mankind are those of God in miniature.

They wind spirally upward, drawing you nearer to the Infinite Perfection that brought you forth into the dawn.

Even as a new-born babe cannot comprehend the parents that gave it form, neither can you understand all that God is or fathom the mighty purpose.

You may gain only approximations and analogies, but within them is a secret door.

Open it when you will, for it reveals to you the importance of your own immortal Soul.

Be still, and hear the whisper that reaches out to you in the silent places.

Fling your innermost self outward into the light of Cosmic Consciousness.

Even a momentary and incomplete glimpse of the Beyond brings peace and strength to the soul.

Contact and know the Source of universal Power.

Harmonize with the greater harmony of Divine Creation.

In one thrilling, breathless moment the Light will filter through the open door, and understanding will come to you.

Receive it for the enlightenment of Men, not for useless wonderment regarding the realm of the Unheard and the Unseen.

The moving Breath of God changes all the multitude of inharmonies into one gigantic, pealing chord as the Great Current flows onward into the arc of evolving Life.

It presses you outward and upward toward the Cosmic Day.

The highest Truths you can bear are available and waiting for all who are steadily and persistently unfolding into the Light.

Listen, then act in harmony with Divine decree.

When you have heard the still, small voice that echoes in the Silence, speak its message in the highways and by-ways of the earth.

Those who are gaining higher realization will understand.

They will know that you are transmuting the base metal of finite thought into the gold of Infinite Spirit: the All Absorbing.

The speed of Cosmic Motion reaches unknowable velocity in the process of creating.

The faint breath of it that fans the earth brings confusion and travail to Men.

Rise above it.

Seek beyond.

Be firm in higher Truth, yet harmonize your will to the Will of God, even as a reed, firm-footed in a bed of shifting sand, bends in yielding to the moving stream.

Those who master Life as it unfolds find chaos and transmute it into order.

They are given sorrow, and transform it into joy.

They receive discord and mold it into harmony.

They absorb violence and fashion it into peace.

The irresistible flood of Becoming sweeps down the jerrybuilt creations of Men.

Yet it bears outward and onward an evolving horde of human souls in the ever-widening stream that is all-powerful and all-enduring.

The mighty creations of the Creator are immortal and everlasting.

The creations of the created are mortal and are for today.

They disappear quickly in the illusory depths of space and time, and are forever lost.

Men struggle desperately in the labor of overcoming.

They fall and rise again, and struggle and fall anew.

They know not that they are wafted onward through the ages by the Great Breath, and they know not whither or how or why.

The finite whirlpools formed in the current of Life are but the tiniest of movements.

They disappear quickly as the stream flows onward to the sea.

All is good and all is necessary for the final emerging of Mankind into the Light.

Chaos precedes consummation, Force precedes Form, even as a yet unmanifested stem and bud must go before the full-blown flower.

The Plan of God is fixed and certain.

All things have their purpose in the slow sweep of moving, evolving Life.

Within the deep Silence you gather creative power.

From it you emerge active and vibrant with joy.

You stand alone and unafraid within the depths of fathomless space, and reach upward toward the mighty consciousness of God.

Have faith.

Labor joyously in the glory that is Creation.

Stand firm on the path.

Be strong and courageous in Truth.

Seek the Silence as you would seek a cooling draught in the stress of desert heat.

Know something of the Infinite Peace of the Great Beyond where all is smooth and orderly in the Divine process of moving and creating and building anew.

Listen to the movement of Cosmic Tides as they sweep onward.

Feel the coming of Change as it emerges out of unformed movement.

Let consciousness be attuned to the Song of Infinite Life.

Know that all is good; all is God.

There is no beginning and no ending.

All has been, all is, and all shall be forever, indestructible and everlasting, in the living, breathing, moving, loving harmony of Divine Creation.

II

The Mystery of Motion

The unchanged and unchangeable **Plan of God,** determines the activity of Creation.

It is formed in the stillness of Cosmic Night, even as your own activity, if it be well balanced and rightly directed, depends upon the strength and inspiration that comes to you when your innermost Being is in repose.

In the Silence you gain the serenity out of which grows the rightful use of Power.

Within the Stillness you receive and form the plan for the sowing.

In action, you scatter abroad the seeds that determine what you shall reap.

Communion within the Silence must be followed by action.

Action should be followed by communion in the Silence.

Each is necessary to the other if you are to prevail in your Divine Mission.

Neglect not the Stillness lest you reap bitter fruit that

grows when unbalanced Force is let loose in the following of a plan half-formed.

After the Stillness, neglect not action lest you sink into the unfathomed pools of stagnation and decay.

Power, if it is to be used for constructive ends, must be directed by a serene and quiet mind.

It is like a sword that is double-edged and of razor sharpness.

It cuts in two directions.

When used unwisely, it sweeps backward to injure the one who does the wielding.

Power is like the pressure of dammed-up waters.

It bursts forth upon the world in a sudden and mighty display.

Unleashed, it is like the lightning that leaps from sky to earth and from earth to sky in the utter abandon of unbalanced Forces.

Under control, it is like a current issuing from a smoothly-running dynamo.

It flows out over prepared channels to give light and heat and sound and motion to Mankind, its ultimate Master.

Power is without limitation within its own sphere, but it must be directed by the gentle hand of Serenity.

It is yours to control and use as a great gift from Cosmic Life. Seek within the Silence for the inspiration that will enable you to use it for the glory of God and the blessing of Mankind.

Power is like a wheel that turns upon itself.

At the outer edge is the eternal warfare between rim and highway, the clashing of atoms against atoms in the breaking down and changing of world forms.

Within the center of the wheel there is no motion.

Here all rests within a deep stillness that never can be disturbed or molested by the warfare of atoms, as they move and change and reform in the tremendous whirling of the outer rim.

Force gains manifestation through circular motion.

This is the Pattern of Things that was conceived and established within the Plan of God: the Divine Idea.

Within the heart of every whirling, all is quiet and orderly in an eternal and never-ending peace.

There is stillness within the howling hurricane.

There is no movement at the center of the maelstrom.

In your quest for Power, seek always the motionless realm that lies within the heart of every turmoil.

In finding the center, you are in the only position where you may control the movement that whirls at the edge of the wheel.

Be still, and learn the secret of creative movement and of created Being as they are whispered to you in the silent places.

Gain the serenity and poise of the advanced soul that is at peace.

Let the Voice yield to you the secrets for which Men have fought and bled and died during all the Ages, as they struggle at the rim of the wheel of evolving Life.

From out of the Silence comes the sighing of a breeze.

It tells of the discontent that lies in restless movement.

It brings the solution to a mystery as it passes by.

It whispers of change, for change is the only certainty that exists within the limitation of the finite realm.

Nothing is motionless.

There is nothing that is fixed.

Life itself is seething with perpetual change as it

surges onward in a planned and ordered movement toward Consummation, the coming into realization of the Plan of God.

Change is the Great Inevitable that arises from creative motion.

Mankind fears it, even as a limpet, clinging to its tiny place upon a rock, dreads the surging of the sea.

Fear not.

Those who fear cannot rise into the Light.

Life fears no change, for its one motion is forward, and it constantly remakes and remolds its endless methods of manifestation.

In changing atoms world forms are built, and they reform anew from atoms new born.

Meet changes as they emerge out of the unformed in a never failing stream.

Expect them, welcome them, glory in them; for thus may you fashion your new-forming atoms so that the pure, white light of Creation may illumine your innermost Being.

It is in perpetual change alone that you find perpetual opportunity.

Heed the voice of the breeze as it tells you the mystery of motion, and also of the Power that motion brings.

Listen while it passes through the stages from the whisper of the zephyr to the shriek of the hurricane, yet zephyr and hurricane alike are but a movement in static air.

All created forms must change, but the basic motion and the substance thereof remain changeless and indestructible through the ages upon ages.

They are the veritable Spirit of God that is moving gently over the face of the Cosmic Sea.

As Serenity is the directing agent of Power, it is to be attained and possessed, not as a treasure on the earth, but as one of Heaven.

In order to gain At-one-ment with the peace and harmony of The Infinite, remain serene and undisturbed within the turmoil and tribulation that lives and breathes and moves at the edge of the wheel.

Be still within the seething, twisting, coiling movements of Men when they are misguided and chaotic.

The perfect control of Power begins with control of yourself.

As you learn of your inherent potentialities, understand also your present limitation.

Use for the glory of God all things within your established sphere, but seek not yet to guide the Cosmic Tides.

Even in the Silence you cannot now understand the song of the stars. The heavenly chords are beyond human comprehension.

Yet you may listen to the gentle melody of unfolding Life as it sings of you and of the mighty Power that you possess.

Gleaming through the blackness of night are the stars.

Beneath you, unfolding into a higher state of Being, are the smallest of Cosmic forms.

Know that each is perfect and all are necessary for the consummation of the Plan of God.

They are fashioned in accordance with that plan by The Omnipotent Hand.

Mastery is the control of each step on the path unfolding before you as you move onward toward realization.

Use for your labor the tools that lie nearest to your grasp.

Know that everything you require is provided.

Begin where you are.

Accept each task as it comes.

Wrestle not with the giants that stand afar on the Way ahead.

To meet them now is to face inevitable failure and defeat.

Use your strength wisely and without fear.

No matter how limited it may seem to you, it is sufficient for the labor of the day.

Be not concerned with the problems of tomorrow.

They lie beyond the veil that obscures the path before you.

Between them and you is the moving mist that never can be pierced or transcended.

The future belongs to God alone.

Listen to the Voice as it whispers to you in all the varied forms and movements of Creation.

Consider the flower, for its message is one of wisdom that is given freely and without price.

From its tiny, unfolding life you may gain a glimpse

of the mystery that lies in the orderly cycle of Divine movement.

Within the heart of a single seed is the static, motionless power of Creation in all its majestic and mighty potentiality.

It is complete, perfect and whole; yet, unvexed by the Infinite Breath, it slumbers within the gloom of Cosmic Night.

With the coming of the Dawn, it stirs and moves and expands in the marvel of growth anew.

A tiny stem pushes into the Light.

A fragment of Life is unfolding that moves in the pattern of the Whole as it presses upward toward the consciousness of **Eternal Being.**

Out of the stem the leaves are born.

Then a bud appears and bursts and grows into a blossom that is fragrant with perfume and glorious with color and light.

Yet halt not here in the gaining of understanding.

The blossom, with all its fragrance and beauty, is not the consummation of moving, changing life.

It is but a passing phase.

The petals wither and die.

The flower fades and returns to the dust.

Darkness weaves the warp and woof of a velvet curtain, and the brightness slowly disappears into the world of the Unformed.

Repose has come after the labor of creating, but the seeds remain.

They are mortal yet immortal, static yet potent, inanimate yet alive.

They rest for a time before bursting forth into the new Day, where all is seething with motion and light as creation moves onward again.

It repeats anew on a vaster scale the melody that was first written and sung within the mighty consciousness of Infinite Life.

Heed the flower as it unfolds before you.

It is a tiny form that gives to all Creation the living fragrance and beauty that it has transmuted from the inanimate substance of rocks and dew.

The path of its unfolding is fixed and planned.

It is identical with the path of the tiniest of atoms and the mightiest of stars.

The stream of Life flows onward forever between widening banks.

It moves and rises and expands in a relentless journey toward the Cosmic Sea.

Nature whispers to you in the Silence.

The mystery of the Ages is yours if you will but heed.

One is all, and All is one.

There is differentiation in expanding motion and varied form, but there can be no separation from the Power that is without beginning and which can never end.

Infinite, creative Life goes onward forever in the Divine cycle of expanding and contracting and expanding anew.

All is sent forth into conscious Being, and all is gathered again home, perfect and complete and full-knowing, for the eternal glory of God, who is the unchanged and unchangeable Source whence all things come.

III

The Way of Love

No one has beheld the countenance of God.

Nor can the finite mind gain understanding either of the plan or the purpose that forms within the consciousness of The Infinite.

You cannot peer into the motionless depths of the Unmanifest. Nor can you sense the potency of the mighty power that rests unmoving within the darkness of the Unformed.

Within your own Being is the complete and final essence of all that is Divine, even as the tiniest drop of water contains the Whole of the rain and hail and snow that descends from the skies, the Whole of rivers and oceans that gather on the earth, and the Whole of the wilderness of ice that moves and rises and breaks upon the surface of the polar seas.

Look above you into star-illumined space if you would understand.

In the blazing darkness you may behold the beauty and majesty of your immortal soul as it lies serene and perfect in the depths of mighty creation.

Within you is the Whole of the Divine that brought you forth from the stillness of eternal night, as the drop of water contains in completeness all that comprises the mightiest of seas.

Desire greatly!

Probe deeply into your own consciousness.

Gain realization of your potential power and of the wonders that Life holds in store for you.

Seek not yet to fathom the mighty consciousness of God that lies within the silent realms of The Absolute.

Begin your search by peering within the depths of your own Being.

Find courage in the making of your quest.

It is the advanced soul alone that pauses to ponder upon the mystery of the Boundless Light.

Why should the Spirit of God move out of darkness into Light in the eternal process of bringing the Unmanifest into manifestation, the Infinite into the finite, the Formless into the formed?

Why should the Great Breath stir within the stillness of unlimited, fathomless space?

Why should Mighty Movement begin, within the

darkness, the vast whirling that is Creation, and continue through the ages upon ages into the light of Cosmic Day?

Wherefore should it press out of the Night into the involuntary arc of Becoming, and move onward through the voluntary arc of conscious Being?

Language that is born of Men can do no more than convey an incomplete and distorted image of Infinite Truth.

Words are feeble things that can be bent and twisted at will.

Those that bring a Divine message to the wise will but pander to the prejudice and misunderstanding of the foolish.

How shall a higher Truth, which is like a soundless and depthless sea, be compressed within the tiny drinking cup of human understanding?

How may the vision of a light that is seen within the darkness be transmuted into thought that can be penned or spoken by Men?

Words fail when you seek to bring the plan or purpose of The Divine into finite comprehension.

Language cannot show you the vastness and completeness of The Infinite, even as it must fail when you seek to picture the glory of a sunrise to those who are blind.

Yet you may believe that all manifestations of Creative Power are good. They are formed in accordance with Infinite Will.

Seek not, therefore, to fathom the depths of Cosmic Mind.

Search for understanding within the simple coilings and twistings and yearnings of Men.

Thus, and thus only, may you behold Divine manifestation in its highest finite form.

The great mystery of Creative Force lies in the secret of its division in order that it may reach manifestation.

All is One which divides into Two, and the Two are the prime creators of all forms; the negative and positive of the realm of Force, the pistil and stamen of the vegetable kingdom, the female and male of the animal, and woman and man of the human.

Every manifestation in form is brought about by the union of two opposites.

As One becomes Two, Two also becomes One.

Herein lies the Divine Principle of Unity, Duality and Trinity, by which Force grows out of the Unmanifest, and Form grows out of Force.

It is thus that the moving Spirit of God becomes the substance and the flesh of the finite world.

The Infinite One is the Creator.

The Two divided Forces are the Creative.

The finite becomes the Created.

Love is the incentive that lives behind all movement and all manifestation.

It is the Divine Spark that kindles into flame a Universe that in the beginning was without form and void, when darkness rested upon the face of the Cosmic Deep.

The love of God is the Infinite Power that causes universal motion.

It presses downward into the densest of earthly form.

Never can you reach a state of Being or an expression of the mystery of Life itself where the love of God is not.

Its potency is like the steam that must come into being before an engine can move.

It is like the salt that is intermingled with the waters of the sea.

Divine love embraces all.

Nothing can escape its irresistible, creative, infinite pressure.

It is the motivation that causes the opposite Forces of Cosmic Creation to join in a continual, joyous, gushing fount of manifestation that is all-enduring and never-ending.

Its power is like that of the lightning that acts without apparent thought, reason or desire when it suddenly transforms the blackness of a midnight sky into the white light of day.

If it were not for Love there would be no Divine Plan.

There could be no movement, no substance and no world manifestation.

Compared with the love of God the loves and hatreds of Mankind are puny things.

Yet they are necessary within the finite realm.

They become momentary, flickering visions of a mighty Force, like a far-off lamp that is mirrored in the darkness of a great deep.

Love gives strength to move, to seize and grasp, to tear apart and destroy.

You express it by the loving of all things unto the uttermost limits of earthly life.

In so doing, you are actuated by the prime incentive that creates the movement and manifestation extending throughout the span of Cosmic Creation.

Mankind bears a relationship to The Infinite which is like that of children to the parents who gave them earthly form.

Of all manifestations of Life that move and breathe and live in the harmony of the Infinite Plan, Man lies nearest to the perfect love of the One that brought all things forth from Cosmic Night.

You approach the realization of that love in ever-widening spirals.

You move with and through The Infinite for a purpose, to a mighty objective: Consummation.

Fulfill your mission joyously.

You occupy a high place in the Divine Scheme of Creation.

The love of God is yours to express.

In a multitude of ways your love becomes a manifestation of The Divine.

God is Love, but it is for you to be loving.

Love is Principle.

It lies deep within the mighty, pulsating heart of creative movement and in all created forms.

To be loving with the Love of God that is all-embracing is a part of your purpose as you rise through the Way of Life into higher realization.

Love presses downward.

It is to be expressed by you on your own level of consciousness, and on those that are beneath you in unfoldment.

In all Creation there is nothing that enables you to gain awareness of the higher realms more quickly and surely than to express Divine Love in selfless service to evolving Life.

The movement of Love is downward, but the path of loving leads upward toward the Light.

You reach it in the worship and adoration of God who created all.

Seek and understand Love.

It is the Great Incentive that exists throughout all Being.

Look above you and about you and beneath you.

Behold the love of God in every creative motion and in all the varied multitude of expressions that appear in created form.

Pressing downward, it reaches the ultimáte when it arises through suffering and self-sacrifice, even as in the love of a mother for her child.

Out of crucifixion she emerges triumphant in the expression of the love of The Divine.

Great is her reward, and swift is her movement toward the Light.

As she peers into the eyes of her new-born babe, her countenance is as radiant as the dawn, as glorious as the summer sky.

Within her heart is the selfless, complete, unreasoning Love from Infinite Life that pours downward upon the just and the unjust in an endless stream.

In the heaven of an infant's eyes she beholds the perfection of The Divine.

In its first cry she hears the whisper of a song that is sung eternally within the realm of the stars.

Love permeates the nethermost depths of finite life and finite form.

Speeding upward in the returning arc, it reaches exaltation in the worship of The Divine.

If you would arise into the pure, flaming, transcending adoration of The Infinite, love Mankind with the passion and the unselfishness of creative Life that never for a moment is stayed, and which can never end.

The love of God sweeps aside all human barriers as it flows downward in the Cosmic Stream.

It cannot be confined within the limitations of man-created custom, institution or decree.

The Force of the Infinite, sent into universal being by the Will of God never can be compressed within finite measures, even as the waters that deluge the earth in the summer rains cannot be held within the tiny vessels that have been formed and fashioned by Men.

Love freely, love deeply, love selflessly, love eternally.

Thus are you obeying the law of The Divine.

Think not that you can love God and despise men.

It is through loving service to all evolving life that you move upward through the higher planes of consciousness toward the mighty realm of the Unmanifest God.

It is the mission of the strong to serve the weak, not for the weak to labor for the strong.

The Master has told you that you are serving Him when you serve the least of these.

Love is the Divine Spark that smolders deep within human consciousness.

When fanned by the Great Breath into flaming creation, it surges over the earth in countless marvels of manifestation.

Out of love for all created things grows the worship of The Creator.

Through selfless service to Men is born true adoration of God.

Communion with The Infinite must begin with the appreciation of all manifest forms that It has made.

Know the wonders of Creation that you may understand the love of God that actuates all Being.

Behold the Unity of everything that moves and lives in a multitude of varying forms.

Neither the heavens nor the earth contain other than has been sent forth by the will and wisdom of The Divine.

In the works of the Creator you behold the glory that is in your own Soul.

You are One with the Divine Principle that creates

and repairs and restores and renews all things within the Cosmic Plan.

No ill can come to you that you have not the power to heal.

Fire cannot burn you.

Sickness cannot strike you down.

Death cannot harm you.

Within the gigantic, moving Stream of Life that flows onward through eternity, there is only Good and only God.

Understand the fullness and the wholeness of the Divine Plan, for thus you can have no vain regrets, nor would you be other than what you are.

You cannot change or improve upon the works of God.

Carry on your mission with gladness.

Use freely the Great Love which has no boundaries and no limitations as it presses downward into every form of Cosmic Life.

Know that its path ultimately leads upward toward an Eternal Peace that never can be disturbed or lessened by the tiny coilings and twistings that become misguided movements of Men.

Find The Infinite in the appreciation of every finite form.

Worship the Highest of All by loving and serving the least of things. God has fashioned them and sent them forth to live and grow and breathe and expand in the glory of Creation that surges onward in the adventure of searching into the Unknown.

It is by loving with the love of God that you fulfill your mission.

Through it you rise upward in consciousness toward the light and the wonders of the Cosmic Day, of which even now you are beholding the Dawn.

IV

The Blinding Light

The pure, white, creative light of Cosmic Day cannot be borne within the finite realm because of its transcendent, illumined radiance.

It must be filtered down through a long series of gradations, like many pairs of colored glasses, that it may come as a soft and modified glow to human eyes.

Men cannot face the Blinding Light of Cosmic Truth.

Nor can they understand other than the simple movements and causes and effects and conclusions that exist within their immediate state of unfoldment and on their particular plane of Being.

A tiny truth must be ascertained and mastered before you may go onward into a higher realization.

Simple problems must be solved before greater problems may be presented.

This is the way of evolving Life.

It is the mystery of the veil of the abyss that lies on the path before you, which recedes and travels with you as you press onward toward the Light.

Consider the utter confusion that would come to the mind of a child should it attempt to master the complexities of higher mathematics while still learning the addition and subtraction of simple numbers.

Yet the small truths it is able to comprehend are marvels upon marvels compared with the knowledge that lies within the consciousness of the vegetable and animal realms.

The child glories mightily in the wonderment of a new and revolutionary understanding.

It believes that it possesses the highest learning.

One of greater knowledge finds difficulty in teaching the expanding, unfolding child that it not yet comprehends all that can be known.

Truth on every plane must be relative until you reach the vast and perfect realm of Cosmic Night: the deep, all-knowing, all-understanding consciousness of the Absolute and Infinite One.

Every truth is a mighty Truth when compared with the knowledge that is within the life of the realms in a lower state of unfoldment. Yet it is but a tiny fragment when contrasted with the understanding of The Infinite, and even of those mighty Souls that have ascended in consciousness to a plane of higher realization.

Even as the den of a fox is but a crude and primitive home in the eyes of men who build their mansions toward the skies, so is the highest understanding of Mankind but a fragmentary and momentary comprehension when compared with that of the Great Ones who have gone onward and upward into the Light.

Whence comes Life?

In what manner and in what form did it first reach the tiny speck of cosmic dust that is called the earth?

How did it affix its multitude of roots therein.

By what method did it first gain visible manifestation?

Such questions have puzzled Mankind since the dawn of human understanding.

The fact that Men are able to ask them and ponder upon them and, after a fashion, to answer them reveals a marvelous unfoldment toward a higher plane of realization.

Of all earthly intelligence, Mankind alone has a concept of God.

Only he is concerned with his relationship to a Higher One.

Thus do Men mightily transcend all other forms of Unfolding Life that move within the earth sphere.

The rocks, the plants, the animals, all of which are evolving deep within the heart of moving, knowing, expanding Intelligence, are concerned only with their tiny existence.

They comprehend nothing of the Cosmic Stream that moves within them and through them and about them.

Neither are they aware of the Great Breath that wafts the mighty current onward in the ever-increasing pressure of growth anew.

Life did not come!

Life is and was and shall be eternally and forever.

In all the mighty realms of Cosmic Stillness and Cosmic Motion, there is no place or condition or state of Being where it is not.

Life did not come to the earth.

It formed and fashioned the earth and laid the foundations thereof.

Life built everything that is within and over and upon the earth.

Finite form is but an expression of evolving consciousness.

The unfoldment of Intelligence comes not as a result of physical change.

Finite improvement grows out of higher states of conscious Being that Life itself must attain in its journey toward the Light of Cosmic Day.

Never can you find a form that is in the process of becoming a higher form.

Never can you find the missing link, for which Men search so vainly.

Basic change takes place within the invisible, silent realm of Cosmic Stillness where a new pattern is determined and the structure of a new form is established.

The manifestation that you behold with finite eyes is but the realization of the basic plan that was formed within the darkness of the Unseen.

It arrives dramatically and fully-created upon the earth.

It is a new expression of Life that has expanded suddenly into a distinct species and a new state of Being.

The higher form has reached unfoldment even as a

butterfly emerges beautiful and new and full-fashioned out of the silence and darkness of the chrysalis.

It goes forth to the conquest of the air even though the caterpillar, which was a lower form of the same evolving Life, could but crawl slowly over the surface of the earth.

Search not for the mystery of evolutionary unfoldment within varying and changing finite form.

You are beholding effects and not causes, results and not transitions.

To know the mystery of Life, seek within the deep stillness of the Unformed, where the Cosmic Tides are moving and changing and expanding into a brighter day.

Understanding comes not from vain inquiry into the seeming confusion of unstable, temporary form.

It lies within the subtile realm of invisible, moving, dynamic, creative Life that journeys onward forever in the restless flowing of the Cosmic Stream.

Search for comprehension of the mystery of Divine Manifestation within the silent darkness of the Soul of Things.

Confuse it not with the animation of finite forms that are visible to human eyes.

All Truth is relative until it reaches deep into the unknowable darkness within the consciousness of the unchanging, unchangeable God.

The quest of Mankind is not for absolute Truth.

It is for a higher truth only, for increased realization leads upward into a more exalted state of Being.

Yet the understanding of individuals among Mankind never can be identical, and never can they agree.

They are not upon the earth in an equal state of unfoldment, nor do they follow the same path.

They are as children of one father and one mother, and are of different ages in the Life Wave of Creation. All are in different degrees of evolutionary growth.

The Great Ones who have trodden the wine-press before you, and are as elder brothers to the children of men, have wrought mightily through the ages in the service of Mankind.

They have spoken all words of every tongue in every land, and have exhausted themselves in their efforts to teach higher Truth to those who are unfolding behind them and beneath them in the great school that is Life.

It is the very simplicity of their teachings that brings confusion to Men who seek blindly and vainly into the illusory depths that are afar from the path to Godlike understanding.

They wander into the dim, uncertain alleys that are beheld with finite vision, whence they can but return again and yet again.

They cross and behold not the path that lies straight and true before them.

They are following false prophets and reflected lights, and are perpetually deceived by a momentary lure of finite things, even as a diver who passes priceless pearls in a vain searching for sunshine and clouds and rain that are reflected into the dark depths of the sea.

The Way toward understanding of higher Truth lies not in wealth and idleness and luxury, nor in the gross pleasures that come from pandering to finite appetites.

It is in the transcendent yet simple joy that arises from labor and love and in the selfless service to your fellow men.

Seek not to gain realization by becoming enmeshed within the spider-web of roads toward the vision of worldly joys.

They but lead into countless turnings and twistings and coilings that return upon themselves and reach again and again the place of starting.

The attainment of treasures on the earth is but a vain pursuit.

It never can be other than a temporary and ephemeral possession that has no value and but little purpose in the flowing of the Cosmic Stream of Life.

It brings to its possessor a multitude of inconveniences and responsibilities that are no more than useless burdens to the enlightened soul.

Envy not any man his possession of wealth or material power, for you comprehend not his difficulties and cares, nor the weariness and hopelessness that come as a reward for searching into the blind alleys of idle pleasure.

Covet not!

You behold only an outward illusion of abundance and happiness.

You know not the secret griefs of those whom you envy.

You see only an appearance that glitters upon a gilded surface, and do not comprehend the sorrows and tears that lie below.

To travel lightly upon the path is the way of wisdom and understanding, for thus are you free from worldly responsibilities that bind you as with chains to your present limited place and station and environment.

The enlightened soul is at liberty to go whithersoever and whenever the spirit leads, into any field that offers opportunity for greater service.

Know that reward inevitably comes from service.

Seek not to render service in order that you may obtain reward.

Wealth is like an anchor to a great ship that is held firmly to an ocean bed.

Only by loosing the chain is the ship free to go on its mission to cities on the far sides of the sea.

Yet, if you are well and sufficiently enlightened, even the burden of riches cannot take from you the treasures of temperance, justice, modesty and love.

Though they increase your cares, they may not rob you of a contented mind and the courage for persistent unfoldment into the Light.

V

The Mystery of Evil

The seemingly unsolvable mystery of Evil lies in the fact of its own non-existence.

All that lives and moves is God, and the goodness of God is a Divine Principle that dominates all Being.

It is the way of Life itself that is flowing onward forever in the Cosmic Tide.

Whatever has the appearance of Evil to the limited understanding of Men is but resistance to the Power of Good.

It is not an independent Force within itself.

Even as failure is not a law, but arises from refusing or neglecting to follow the Law of Success, so is evil not a power or the result of a Divine decree.

It is like a dam that is constructed to prevent the waters of a river from flowing onward to the sea.

For a fleeting moment it seems potent and powerful, and those who judge from the appearance of things believe that it can prevail and has prevailed.

Yet the river rises steadily and soon flows onward unchecked.

The dam is turned into an instrument for good, for out of seeming evil comes irrigation and power and light to Men.

Every form of evil can be transmuted into Good if you but overcome it with the greater Force of selfless service to Mankind, for the way of Love is the expanding, potent, powerful glory which belongs to God alone.

Resist not evil within its own sphere.

Overcome all with the positive, dynamic Force of Good that moves onward irresistibly in the pressure of Cosmic Creation that can never be stayed.

By means of love, service and forgiveness you may overcome evil and wrong and fancied wrong.

All are within the power of the omnipotent, omnipresent Breath of God that cannot be transcended or turned backward or destroyed.

Even as the mighty and misguided strength of the wild elephant is turned into the service of Men, so the way of evil can be transformed into eternal good.

Overcome evil by following the way of Love, which is also the way of Mercy.

It is reached in forgiveness and understanding and compassion and selfless service.

No matter how insignificant and unimportant such things may seem to you, it is through them that you gain the treasures of heaven, for they are eternal and immortal and never can be lost.

The pursuit of treasures on the earth is but to scatter your precious strength and Godlike power abroad in the attempted attainment of an aimless and an idle dream.

You cannot hold them in your grasp.

They are like sunbeams and moving shadows that vanish with the coming of the night.

Eternal values lie only in the attainment of things that neither can be bought nor sold.

They are not of the finite world.

Probe deeply into the peaceful realm of the Silence, and a Voice will whisper to you the secrets of the Ages if you will but heed.

Understand the way of love and forgiveness. Follow it persistently.

It is the shining, illumined path that leads upward into the Blinding Light.

71

When you have found it you may know that your journey onward into the vast Unknown will be swift and sure.

It is one of gladness and peace and ever-increasing joy.

The path of Love is never one of contraction or renunciation.

It is a continual expansion within the heart of the mighty, flowing Stream of Life.

Following it does not involve the sacrifice of what is of value to you.

There is no other sacrifice than to lay down the seeming good in order to take up something of greater worth.

You cast aside a fragment of glass to seize a lovely jewel.

You lay down a burden of stones that you may take up a purse of gold.

Out of love comes forgiveness before forgiveness is asked, including all the wrongs and fancied wrongs that Men and the children of Men have done to you.

Nothing other than forgiveness is possible when you

gain the higher understanding that leads toward the Light.

The desire to punish and torture others is the way of primitive, child-like man.

To forgive is the way of Mastery.

It arises out of a true comprehension and use of the perfect love of The Infinite.

To hold and nurture thoughts of punishment and vengeance is but a turning away from the current of the Stream that bears you onward into a higher realization.

You become lost in the countless eddies and whirlings that twist and turn ever and again upon themselves.

Seek not to prevail in your mission on the earth through punishment of your weaker brothers.

It is by following the way of love and mercy and for-giveness that you overcome evil and reach the Blinding Light.

Why should Men desire to punish Men?

To gain pleasure or satisfaction by causing pain to another is but returning to a sadistic past that lives deep within subconscious memory.

It is a forbidden thing that belongs to a dark and forgotten age when Mankind was emerging into the dawn of conscious Being.

The weaker brothers who are behind you and beneath you in evolutionary unfoldment are bound to you forever in your journey into the Unknown.

Never can you depart afar from them, nor can you escape your responsibilities concerning them.

You are all of one family, children of the Eternal One.

The way upward is found in selfless love.

You reach it when you love passionately and constantly and eternally.

Thus you show a perfect faith in Mankind, and in your own high place in the Great Plan.

Though you are scorned by Men, and though you are used wrongfully and despitefully by them, even by such trials and overcomings are you exalted.

In their situation, could you have done better than they?

Even so, why should you desire to add to the sorrows and sufferings and tears of those who are weaker than you?

Love, and despise not!

See the good and not the evil.

Teach by example.

Do not condemn.

Know that those whom you would instruct are as children in unfoldment.

They have learned but few of the lessons that Life alone can teach them.

There are no words so beautiful and inspiring as those of appreciation and love.

There can be no tongue as eloquent as a friendly smile.

The younger learns but little from the elder.

The elder gains knowledge from the courage and original thinking of the young.

Life is in a continual state of flux.

It is moving and changing in a creative stream where all things are again and again made new.

The Spirit of Youth is in close touch with the changing thought and purpose of Things as they sweep slowly out of the realm of Cosmic Night.

Harbor not thoughts of hatred and vengeance.

Think not that you can punish your younger brothers, or force upon them your way of life.

75

You only retard the speed of your own journey into the Unknown.

Learn well the commandment, You shall not kill.

Then may you be given the realization of a higher truth, You cannot kill.

Life is eternal and never-ending, and you cannot injure another.

Your power to harm ends with injury to yourself.

Punishment must come to every form of Life that ignores or disobeys or misinterprets Divine Law.

Leave all to God, nor seek to change or improve upon The Infinite Plan.

The Cosmic Cycle moves eternally in an endless spiral.

It reaches new evolutionary heights at the completion of each movement.

The end of one cycle is but the beginning of another.

As night follows day, and as winter follows summer, a new kindliness comes now upon an earth that has been torn with cruelty and hatred and avarice for countless years.

It is a voluntary turning away from darkness, even as the maw-crammed beast must abandon its kill to find solace in rest and sleep.

The everlasting Light shall shine no more where Men, because of blinded eyes, behold it not.

They shall seek the Way of God gladly, eagerly, even as a sorrowing child seeks a mother's arms.

The deep voice of the Silence whispers a great expansion outward that follows the long searching for spiritual attainment in the possession of dust.

Men are beginning to heed the message of the Ages that has been told to them of the Way, the one and only Way, the Way into the Blinding Light.

From very weariness they faint in their long, fruitless struggle of resisting the power of the Cosmic Stream.

They have exhausted themselves in an unavailing inhumanity of Man to Man.

Their tiny playhouses, that were erected in selfishness and greed, have collapsed upon their heads.

The foundations were of dust and could not withstand the blows of men striking men.

The house fell, for it was built upon shifting sands.

It fell, for it was erected by pride and greed and fear.

It was a house divided against itself.

Weep not for these sorrowing children because their

jerrybuilt creations have fallen in the storms of their own creating.

They shall be cared for tenderly.

They shall be comforted.

Their tears shall be wiped away.

Their wounds will be washed and healed by those who love them and understand.

Punishment is theirs, but punishment is merely the reward that comes from misunderstanding and wrong-doing.

Their playthings shall be taken away for a time until they learn to use them without injuring one another.

Within the Silence they shall meditate upon their troubles and sufferings.

Then shall they return with greater knowledge and a higher realization.

Playthings once more shall be theirs.

They shall dwell in peace, taking delight in companionship one with the other.

They shall find happiness and joy in sharing the treasures of the earth, for only thus can treasures be possessed.

VI

Adoration

Deep within the unfathomed seas of the Stillness, I touch the hem of the robe of Eternal Night.

I brush against the dark veil that hangs motionless before the vast mystery of the Unformed.

I listen to the music of Unborn Ages that resounds within the unprobed recesses of the mighty Unknown.

Spirit of Infinite Harmony!

O Etheric Chords that form and breathe and quiver beyond the realm of the stars!

In you I hear the Theme of themes, the Melody of melodies, the Song of songs, the never-diminishing Chorus that is the spirit of growth, the glory of Life, and the eternal Power of the whispering Silence; the song that echoes forever within the unfathomed depths; the song of a Soul.

In the Stillness I attune consciousness high into the movement of the Great Breath which stirs the Etheric Realms with vibrations of Infinite Music that resound forever into the vast confines of star-illumined, Cosmic Day.

All is mine!

Mine is the kingdom of the earth.

Mine is the Great Power.

Mine is the Divine Glory.

Mine is the limitless, Infinite Harmony that breathes through the ages upon ages its loving, living Light into the unformed stillness of Eternal Being.

In the silent watches of the night I hear the Voice, the whispering Voice, the magic Voice, the breathing, resounding, creative Voice that echoes within the dark, unbounded corridors of the Etheric Beyond.

It is the voice of the Silence that transcends all limitations of space and time and motion, as it sounds within the mighty depths of Infinite Consciousness.

It whispers softly into my dreaming.

It calls, and I must arise!

It summons me out of the slumber of the ageless Ages, and I follow the call outward and upward into the glory of the Blinding Light.

In the still whisper that vibrates within the mystic tones of cosmic viols, in the spoken chords from the harp strings of etheric movement, in the blare of the brazen trumpets of Divine Manifestation, and in the rolling crash of the mighty drums of Infinite Being, I behold the transcendent chorus of the Great Song.

I leap upward toward the Light, and even as I begin to grasp the secret of the eternal harmony, it fades away into the depths of a Great Stillness, for it yet must remain the Unknown.

O rustling whisper of Creation that breathes softly within the darkness of Eternal Night!

O mighty Voice that thunders within the white and blinding light of Cosmic Day!

With your Divine Harmony resounding forever into my Soul, I ascend toward the vast heights of transcendent illumination.

I travel faster than the speed of thought.

I go farther than the farthest star.

I search into the outermost confines of Cosmic Creation.

I pause and hear the rustle of the robe of Eternal Darkness moving and breathing and whispering within the unknown Void: the deep, silent and fathomless oceans of Unformed Life.

I lift my vision to the splendor that lies in all the works of The Infinite as they form within the movement of boundless Creation.

From them I seek understanding of the power and purpose and glory of my own immortal Being.

Even as the flaming comet wanders afar into the etheric beyond and returns ever and anon to the sun in its proper time, so I return again and again to the realization of the Eternal One.

I seek and find the glory in the beholding of all that has been fashioned by the Mighty Omnipotent Hand.

Who but God could have builded so bountifully and so magnificently throughout the vastness of Cosmic Creation?

What but Infinite Wisdom and Power could have formed the wonders that move within the earth and without the earth in continuous and orderly unfoldment?

The heavens are full of beauty and grandeur beyond the understanding of Men.

They are peopled with an awe-inspiring array of worlds and stars.

Yet all were formed from the tiniest of things, even as those that exist upon the earth.

The smallest of atoms is but a miniature pattern of the marvels that dwell within the depths of the skies.

Alike they are proclaiming the greatness and the glory

of the Infinite One, for less than Omnipotence could not have created them, nor could have fashioned even the least that is among them.

Mighty, O mighty are the stars that gleam within the blackness of never-ending space!

Marvelous is their light, for they are suns beyond the sun.

Even as the particles of Force that comprise the atom whirl about the still, unmoving nucleus, even as the planets move through their orbits with perfect precision and in perfect time, so do the stars circle about a central Light that transcends all suns and stars as the smallest among them transcends a candle gleaming within the night.

What but God could have set them in their prescribed courses?

Who but The Infinite could have formed them for Its mighty purpose, in accordance with Its Plan?

I behold the Hand of the Creator within the earth, in the grasses and the wilderness of blossoms that carpet the fields, in the trees that lift their heads within the forest and along the borders of the stream, and in all the manifestations of Life that are within my vision and my comprehension.

Within and without is the wonder of growing, expanding Movement in the eternal process of unfolding into higher conscious Being.

The beasts dwell content within their tiny realm, the birds soar afar into the skies, even the worms burrow in the sheltering earth.

They feel that they exist, but wonder not at their tiny life, nor do they behold the glory that is among the stars.

They rejoice in the pleasure of their simple existence, but they know not whence they came nor how nor why nor whither they shall go.

With unconscious Being they move within the silent stream of evolving Life.

Not in a thousand years is there the loss of a single species as generation unfolds into succeeding generation.

The wonders within wonders that lie in all creative Force and created Being proclaim the greatness and the glory of the Mighty One; Divine Creation.

It commands the grasses and the flowers to spring up in their season.

It orders the stars in their courses.

It has decreed my Being and my Life, and every labor

and responsibility that is mine lies within the vast consciousness of the Infinite One.

My soul arises upward into the realization of All.

I behold the finite manifestations of the Creator in order that I may know the path and the plan of Creation.

Even so do I become exalted!

Enfolded within the soft depths of the Silence, I sink into the mighty realm of the skies.

I wander into the mystic, cloud-robed heights of The Beyond.

I travel from star to star in my eternal quest.

I grope to find the Blinding Brightness that springs full-formed out of the Unknown.

I touch ever and again the misty veil that lies across the path into the still and motionless realm of the Unmanifest God.

When will I reach the Great Realization?

In what manner will I acquire the pure consciousness that enfolds into the Limitless Light?

When may I gain the supreme Illumination that is beyond the awareness of finite earth?

What matters such minute things?

What can be so unimportant in the Plan of God as the finite concept of time?

It is as an imaginary drop of water lost within the depths of an imaginary sea.

It fades into ungraspable nothingness as I turn within the Silence that lies deep and still in my innermost Being.

All is One, and One is All.

Time is enfolded into the darkness and the light of Divine Movement, and is no more.

It is lost within the Oneness of the Eternal.

It becomes merged within the cosmic cycle that has no measurement, for it is the beating of the mighty heart of Creation.

I go upward on the path quickly or slowly as I choose to go.

Time is absorbed into the potential of my Infinite yet finite Will.

To me is given the glory of the earth with its majestic and limitless beauty.

Mine is the perfect exaltation that is the final heritage of the finite world.

Mine is the realm of the skies.

I look upward to find an answer in the gray of early morn.

It moves and expands and grows.

I behold the blazing brightness of the rising sun.

Within the great light of noon I stand when all Nature sings the glory of God in the blinding rays that sweep the sky.

Slowly the light moves onward toward the darkness.

I am one with the peace and beauty of the dying day.

The low sun sinks into the mantle of purple and gold that lies behind the curtain of eternal hills.

Twilight forms out of the blazing sunset.

The dim light reaches slowly into the dark void of the night and the stars.

Time is no more.

It is but a finite concept of the cyclic movement of Creation, and dark, unlimited Space is but the mighty body of the Infinite One.

All is within the consciousness of God. Creative movement goes onward as the Unformed reaches manifestation, and Night becomes Day.

I behold the stillness and the peace of winter when Nature sleeps.

I see it awake in the warmth of the sun.

It stirs and moves and expands into a glory of summer green.

The earth puts forth in the wonder of eternal growth, and joins in the mighty chorus of praise.

Even as noon passes into twilight and night, the green beauty of summer merges again into the brown of the reaping time, and into the still whiteness of winter sleep.

The cycle of Infinite Movement goes onward forever throughout the vast realm of creation.

The Great Breath moves outward and inward again.

I behold the mystery of Eternal Life in the cycle of earthly things.

I see it in the brightness of day, and in the midnight blackness and stillness that is alive with the light of expanding, growing stars.

Alone in the Silence the song within my soul is attuned to the harmony of the night.

All is peace; the peace of God, the peace of The Infinite One that moves forever in the wonders of Cosmic Creation.

In the deep Stillness I hear the call that echoes out of the boundless depths beyond the realm of time and space and finite thought.

It is a clear, irresistible call from within to arise and behold the glory of the Divine.

It is a Call from afar.

Spirit of Eternal Youth!

O Divine and Ageless cycle of sentient growth that lives and moves and expands and returns to the beginning, again and again fashioning all things anew!

Whither away on your adventure into the Unknown? You cannot rest, for you are Divine Movement.

You cannot sleep, for you must learn of the wonders that lie beyond the dark hills of unformed Life.

You do not meditate upon the future, nor fear whatever it may hold for you.

You wonder not at the Cause of Things, nor of whither your joyous movement will take you.

The wind whispers as you pause with head uplifted.

You listen to the song of birds and the trees, and to the great hush of breathing, growing things.

The Spring is upon you and a great glory is in your heart.

O laughing Youth, you are the mighty movement of Creation!

You are the living, breathing essence of the Divine, for God is ever young.

Within the realms of Creative Motion there is only youth; youth that moves and grows and unfolds, and is unchanged in the eternal renewing into youth again.

There can be nothing that is aged.

There is no growing old.

Within the mighty Plan of God there is only the re-forming and changing into the new.

I am eternally young, for I am the spirit of Youth.

I am an ever-new Soul expanding within the gigantic, incomprehensible Cosmic Stream that flows onward and changes and reforms and refashions, yet moves forever toward its goal of Consummation.

I behold the new glory that is within me and without.

I listen to the buzzing of a bee and the whisper of a flower.

I hear the tiny mole beneath the surface of the earth pushing its way amidst the roots of living, growing things.

I hear the song of birds.

I see the dawn, the day, the evening, and the still, lovely night.

Within me lives and moves the spirit of Eternal Youth.

Never can I be old!

Why have you hidden beyond my sight, O Limitless Light of the Unknown?

I have sought you vainly in the dark dwelling house of the Beyond.

I have searched for you and called to you and yearned for you through the vast ages.

Why have you remained behind the veil with your scintillating brightness hidden from my eyes?

For long Eons have I been lost in darkness.

My soul has cried aloud for you.

I have searched among the myriad Suns that gleam within the vast confines of outer space.

I have groped within the dark halls of Etheric Unrest.

I have descended into the depths of the Cosmic Seas that lie in the still realms of Infinite Movement.

I have ventured into the borders of the world of the Unformed.

I have brushed against the robe of Eternal Night.

Yet I found you not, O light of Cosmic Understanding. My soul has become wearied with vain searching.

With bowed head and humbled heart I have resigned myself.

I await your call.

Out of the still, gray dawn comes the song of a bird.

The morning turns into rose and to gold.

At my feet rests a living, growing, moving carpet of flowers.

The trees lift their glory to the sky.

The sun appears in the flaming, flashing splendor of day.

I stand within the heart and bosom of God!

The mighty song of Creation is resounding in the skies, and in the earth.

It is the song of my own Soul.

I lift my eyes to the serene, unmoving hills.

I thank God for all that I am, for the privilege of living, for the glory of thinking and understanding and Being.

My power is that of the Angels.

I am a child of God coming into my mighty inheritance.

The Great Beyond is the Great Within.

O Divine Creator of All!

Mighty Breath that presses outward in irresistible movement!

I am a vital part in the Great Plan.

Within me is the Oneness of All.

When I am I you cannot be You.

It is only when I am not that You are.

To find All I must cease to be I.

Thus do I gain the realization that I am in You and with You and of You.*

Thus may I behold the Limitless Light.

Thus may I sing the eternal song of the soul.